DI031887

Explore the Universe

STARS—
THE INSIDE STORY

WORLD
BOOK

a Scott Fetzer company
Chicago
www.worldbookonline.com

World Book, Inc.
233 N. Michigan Avenue
Chicago, IL 60601
U.S.A.

For information about other World Book publications, visit our Web site at **http://www.worldbookonline.com** or call **1-800-WORLDBK (967-5325)**.

For information about sales to schools and libraries, call **1-800-975-3250 (United States)**, or **1-800-837-5365 (Canada)**.

Library of Congress Cataloging-in-Publication data

Stars-- the inside story.
   p. cm. -- (Explore the universe)
   Includes index.
   Summary: "An introduction to stars with information about their age, size, colors, and other characteristics. Includes diagrams, fun facts, glossary, resource list, and index" --Provided by publisher.
   ISBN 978-0-7166-9547-9
   1. Stars--Juvenile literature. I. World Book, Inc.
   QB801.7.S726 2010
   523.8--dc22

                        2009042578

ISBN 978-0-7166-9544-8 (set)
Printed in China by Leo Paper Products, LTD.
   Heshan, Guangdong
1st printing February 2010

Cover Illustration:
Tiny grains of dust in the Witch Head Nebula reflect blue light from the bright star Rigel (center), which shines 40,000 times as brightly as the sun. At the end of its life, Rigel will likely explode. The shock wave that follows will cause dust and gas in the Witch Head Nebula to collapse, forming new stars.

NASA/STScI Digitized Sky Survey/Noel Carboni

CONTENTS

If a word is printed in **bold letters that look like this,** that word's meaning is given in the glossary on pages 60-61.

INTRODUCTION

The stars that illuminate Earth's darkened skies have been described as "pinholes in the veil of night." For tens of thousands of years, people marveled at their beauty but could only guess about their true nature. Were they really holes in the sky? Were they signs from the gods?

With the invention of the telescope, scientists began to explore the scientific nature of these glowing balls, including the sun, our star. Today, ever more powerful telescopes, both on Earth and in space, are giving scientists remarkable insights into the ways stars are born, live, and die. Yet many mysteries remain.

A burst of new, bright blue stars is captured in an image from the Hubble Space Telescope. Star formation occurs in regions of gas and dust called nebulae, such as this one named NGC 3603.

ENERGY FACTORIES

The sun is a **star**, one of billions in the Milky Way Galaxy. Much of the energy *emitted* (given off) by the sun and other stars is in the form of light we can see, known as **visible light.** The heat we feel on our skin from the sun is another form of energy called **infrared light**. The energy that tans our skin is an invisible form of energy called **ultraviolet light.** Stars may also emit **X rays, radio waves,** and other forms of energy. In fact, many stars produce all the forms of **electromagnetic radiation**, both visible and invisible, in the **spectrum.** This energy travels through space as particles called **photons.** Photons travel at the speed of light—about 186,282 miles (299,792 kilometers) per second.

CLASSIFYING STARS

Stars vary in size, one of the characteristics astronomers use to classify these glowing objects. They also vary in **mass** (amount of matter) and brightness. In addition, stars range in color from reddish to bluish, depending on their surface temperature.

SOCIAL STARS

Stars typically form groups, which may range in number from a few tens to a few millions. Collections of these groups are found in **galaxies,** the building blocks of the universe. The sun and the **solar system** belong to the Milky Way Galaxy. On a clear night, part of our galaxy can be seen as a glowing, whitish band of light stretching across the sky.

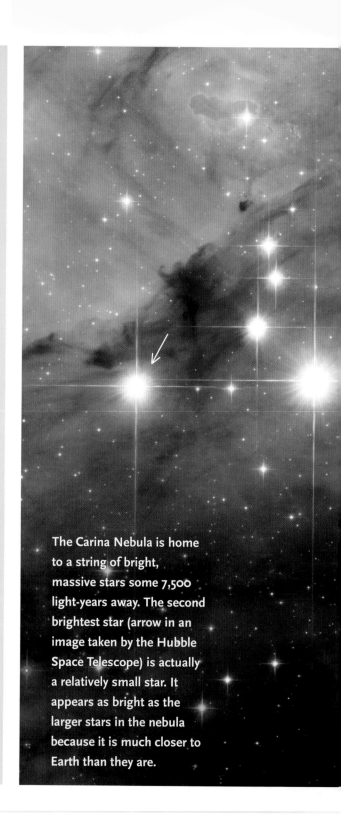

The Carina Nebula is home to a string of bright, massive stars some 7,500 light-years away. The second brightest star (arrow in an image taken by the Hubble Space Telescope) is actually a relatively small star. It appears as bright as the larger stars in the nebula because it is much closer to Earth than they are.

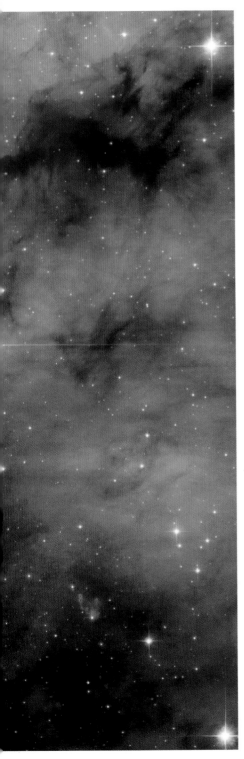

DID YOU KNOW?

There are fewer grains of sand on all of Earth's beaches than there are stars in the universe.

Rigel is a massive star located in the constellation Orion (the Hunter), about 722 light-years from Earth. The star represents the left foot of the hunter.

THE IMPORTANCE OF MASS

Stars give off light and heat while **planets** do not because of their **mass** (amount of matter). The only way an object in space can become a star is by collecting a vast amount of matter. Even Jupiter, the largest planet in the **solar system,** did not collect enough matter as it was forming to become a star.

Stars produce energy through **nuclear fusion** reactions. In a fusion reaction, the *nuclei* (cores) of two atoms join together, creating a new nucleus. Fusion converts nuclear matter into energy. Fusion can occur only when an object in space reaches sufficient **mass** to have intense **gravity.** The force of gravity increases the pressure and heat in the **core** of the object. Eventually, the pressure and heat become great enough for fusion to occur. When an object is able to sustain nuclear fusion reactions in its core, we call it a star.

The crescent moon and the planet Venus—the bright object to the lower right of the moon—are visible in Earth's night sky because they reflect light from the sun. They do not give off their own visible light.

DID YOU KNOW?

Several million stars have been named. Of those, about 200 to 300 were named by people in ancient times, mainly by the Arabs and the Romans.

SQUEAKING BY

As huge as the sun is, it is not a large star. It has only a modest amount of mass and gravitational force. Astronomers have found *celestial* (heavenly) objects that appear to be failed stars. These objects, called **brown dwarfs,** are many times as massive as Jupiter. However, they did not collect enough matter as they were forming to become stars. Unlike the sun, they are not able to sustain nuclear fusion.

Brown dwarfs, such as TWA 5b (below, center), are believed to be failed stars. Although brown dwarfs are many times smaller than the sun, they are typically 15 to 75 times as massive as the planet Jupiter.

Jupiter

Brown dwarf
TWA 5b

Sun

HOW MANY STARS ARE THERE?

COUNTING STARS

A person standing outside on a clear night, far from the lights of a city, can see as many as 3,000 stars. But this number is a tiny fraction of the billions of stars in the Milky Way alone. To try to count the stars in the universe, astronomers map the visible stars in one section of the sky. They then use a formula to estimate how many dimmer stars there are for each of the visible stars. Finally, they multiply the total estimated number of stars in a region by the number of sections in the sky.

Counting the stars is difficult for other reasons. Astronomers cannot see all the stars and galaxies in even one section of the sky, even with the most powerful telescopes on Earth or in space. Some are hidden by vast clouds of dust and gas. Others are too far away. In addition, some distant galaxies appear only as single blurs of light. Determining the size and brightness of a galaxy

The star cluster NGC 290 is a region of newly formed stars. The cluster is found in the Small Magellanic Cloud, a galaxy located just outside the Milky Way.

The universe appears to have many more stars than astronomers had previously believed, according to data collected by NASA's Galaxy Evolution Explorer space probe. Scientists had previously estimated that there were about 500 small stars for every 1 massive star. The Explorer probe revealed that there are at least 2,000 small stars for each massive star.

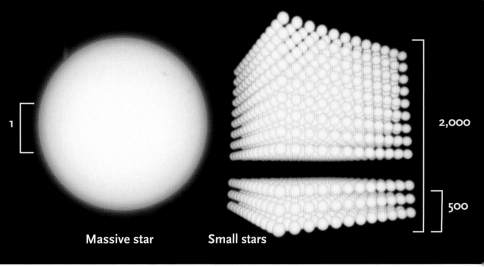

Massive star   Small stars

gives astronomers only a rough estimate of the number of stars it contains. Stars are born and die, so the number of stars in any galaxy changes over time. Finally, the starlight we see in the night sky may have been traveling through space for billions of years. The stars that emitted that light may no longer exist.

WHAT'S A SEXTILLION?

Despite these challenges, astronomers have arrived at an estimate of the number of stars. In 2003, a team of scientists in Australia and Scotland estimated that the universe has 70 sextillion stars. That number represents a 7 followed by 22 zeros—70,000,000,000,000,000,000,000. However, this number represents only stars visible to telescopes. In fact, the number of stars in the universe is probably unknowable.

DID YOU KNOW?

If you could stack 70 sextillion pieces of paper one on top of the other, the pile would be long enough to extend to the sun and back to Earth 19 million times.

A STAR IN THE MIDDLE

The sun dominates even the largest **planets** in the **solar system.** The sun's **mass** (amount of matter) is about 1,000 times as great as that of Jupiter, the largest planet. In the Milky Way, fewer than 5 percent of **stars** are brighter or more massive.

Nevertheless, compared with all other known stars, the sun is not very large. A distant star called Antares, for example, is about 700 times as wide as the sun. In fact, astronomers classify the sun as a **dwarf star** because other kinds of stars are so much bigger.

Compared with the smallest stars, however, the sun is a giant. These stars, called **neutron stars,** have a radius of only about 6 miles (10 kilometers). (The radius is the distance from the center of a circle or sphere to the outer edge.) The sun's radius is 432,000 miles (695,500 kilometers).

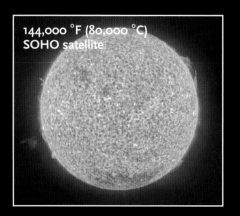

144,000 °F (80,000 °C)
SOHO satellite

1,800,000 °F (1,000,000 °C)
TRACE satellite

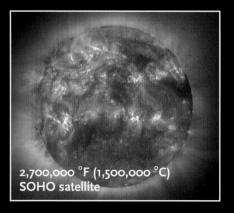

2,700,000 °F (1,500,000 °C)
SOHO satellite

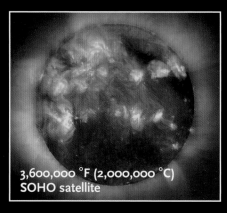

3,600,000 °F (2,000,000 °C)
SOHO satellite

Information about the temperatures of different gases in the sun's *corona* (outer layer) is revealed in images taken at different wavelengths of ultraviolet light. Such information allows scientists to study the composition of the corona.

The sun is an average-size star, compared with other known stars. It is also rather average in terms of its brightness and temperature.

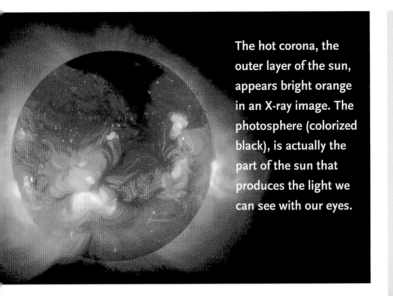

The hot corona, the outer layer of the sun, appears bright orange in an X-ray image. The photosphere (colorized black), is actually the part of the sun that produces the light we can see with our eyes.

The sun is also rather ordinary in terms of its temperature and brightness. Some stars are more than 100,000 times as bright as the sun. In contrast, some stars are less than 1/10,000 as bright. There are hotter stars, which are much bluer than the sun, and cooler stars, which are much redder.

ON ITS OWN

The sun is somewhat unusual among the stars of the Milky Way in one way. Most of the known stars in the galaxy belong to a type of star system called a **binary system**. In a binary system, two stars hold each other captive by the force of **gravity,** and each one orbits the other. Scientists think that from 50 to 75 percent of all stars are members of a binary system.

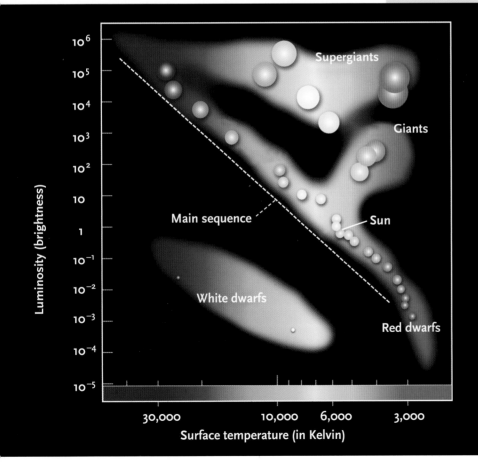

A Hertzsprung-Russell diagram enables astronomers to show the relationship between the temperature and *luminosity* (brightness) of stars.

WHY DOES THE SUN LOOK DIFFERENT FROM OTHER STARS?

DISTANCE AND PERSPECTIVE

In the daytime sky, the sun is a big yellow ball. In the night sky, other stars—even those larger than the sun—appear as mere points of light. Distance and perspective explain this difference. Perspective is the effect of distance on the way we see things. On a road at night, the headlights of cars coming from the opposite direction seem to get bigger as they get closer. Headlights in the far distance, however, look much smaller. In a similar way, perspective affects how we see our relatively close sun and far distant stars. The nearest star to the solar system is about 270,000 times as far from the sun as Earth is from the sun.

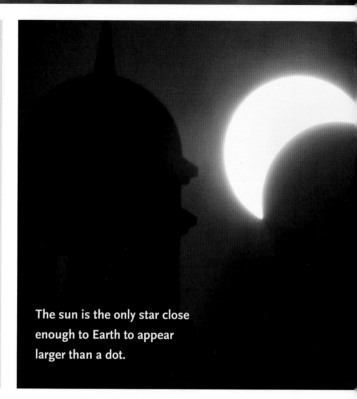

The sun is the only star close enough to Earth to appear larger than a dot.

The sun, Earth, and Venus appear together in an image taken by the Voyager 1 spacecraft in 1990 from a distance of 4 billion miles (6.4 billion kilometers)—beyond the orbit of Pluto. The sun appears much larger than it actually is because of the glare from sunlight on the camera.

Venus

Earth

A MATTER OF PERSPECTIVE

Distance and perspective also explain why the moon appears to be nearly as large as the sun. The sun is about 400 times as large in size as the moon. But the sun is also about 400 times farther away from Earth than the moon. As a result, from Earth, the sun and the moon appear about the same size.

DAYTIME ON NEPTUNE

Neptune is farther from the sun than any other **planet** in the **solar system**—about 30 times farther than Earth. From Neptune, the sun would look like a bright star in a black sky. In contrast, from the surface of Mercury, the planet closest to the sun, the sun would appear as a giant yellow ball, much larger than it does from Earth.

The sun appears as nothing more than a bright point of light when viewed from the dwarf planet Sedna in this artist's illustration. Sedna is the farthest known object in the solar system. It is about 8 billion miles (13 billion kilometers) from Earth and three times as far from the sun as Neptune.

HOW FAR AWAY ARE THE STARS?

THE SPEED OF LIGHT

Light travels through space at about 186,282 miles (299,792 kilometers) per second. In the time required to read that last sentence, a light ray from the sun can travel several million miles through space. The distance between the sun and Earth is about 93 million miles (150 million kilometers). It takes a light ray from the sun slightly more than 8 minutes to reach Earth.

LIGHT-YEARS

The distance that light travels in one year is known as a **light-year.** This distance is approximately 5.88 trillion miles (9.46 trillion kilometers). Distances to **stars** are usually measured in light-years.

Proxima Centauri, the nearest star to the sun, is about 4.2 light-years away. If astronauts could fly there in a spaceship traveling at a speed of 1,000 miles (1,600 kilometers) per hour, it would take about 2.8 million years to reach the star.

Many stars, however, are so far away that it takes their light millions or even billions of years to reach Earth. When we look at stars in the night sky, we are actually seeing star history. We have no way of knowing what is happening right now on very distant stars. When the light leaving those stars now finally reaches this region of space, the sun and Earth may no longer even exist.

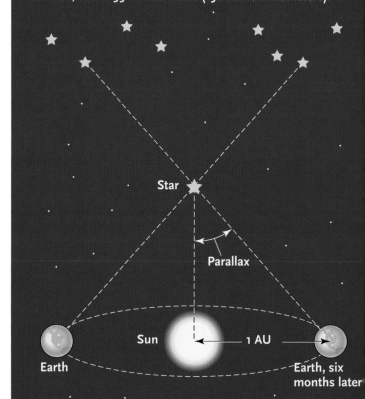

Astronomers use a measurement called parallax to determine distances to the nearest stars. Parallax is the difference in the angle of a star's location in the sky when viewed from two points in Earth's orbit. One AU (astronomical unit) is the average distance from the sun to Earth, about 93 million miles (150 million kilometers).

DID YOU KNOW?

Sirius, the brightest star in Earth's night sky, is one of the few stars named by the ancient Greeks. "Sirius" means "scorcher" in the Greek language.

Except for the sun, all stars are so far away from Earth that it takes their light at least several years to reach us.

The light we see today from a galaxy known as NGC 908 left that galaxy about 65 million light-years ago, when dinosaurs still walked the Earth.

BINARY STARS—
SEEING DOUBLES

Most of the stars in the universe seem to travel with a companion—unlike the sun, whose closest neighbor is several light-years away. The second and third closest stars to the sun, Alpha Centauri A and B, are part of a *binary* (two-star) system. Two stars are considered part of a binary system if they orbit each other. Some binary pairs can be closer to each other than Earth is to the sun. Others may be many times farther apart than the planet Neptune and the sun. Some pairs may contain one or more unusual stars, such as a neutron star or a black hole. Astronomers have even found systems of stars that contain three stars. As many as half of the "individual" stars we see in the night sky are actually two stars in a binary system.

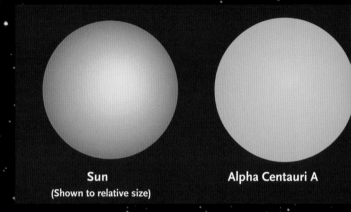

Sun
(Shown to relative size)

Alpha Centauri A

▲ The three stars in the Alpha Centauri star system (above) are Earth's closest stellar neighbors. Alpha Centauri A and Alpha Centauri B are binary stars that orbit each other. Proxima Centauri, the closest of the three, may be bound by gravity to its larger neighbors, but scientists are unsure to what degree.

The binary star Albireo (above), which is about 380 light-years away in the constellation Cygnus (the Swan), appears to be a single bright star to the unaided eye.

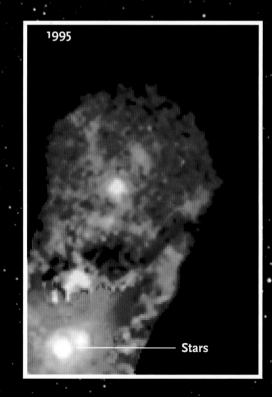

1995

Stars

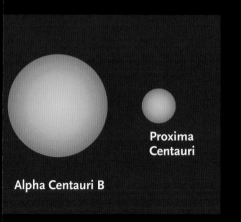

Proxima
Centauri

Alpha Centauri B

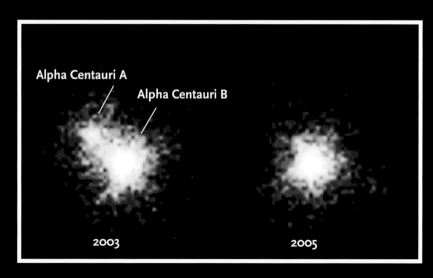

Alpha Centauri A

Alpha Centauri B

2003

2005

▲ Alpha Centauri A may have periods of low light activity. In
an X-ray image taken in 2003 (above, left), the star appears
as a dimmer companion to Alpha Centauri B. In an image
taken in 2005 (above, right), Alpha Centauri A seems to
have disappeared. The reason for the change in brightness
is being investigated by astronomers.

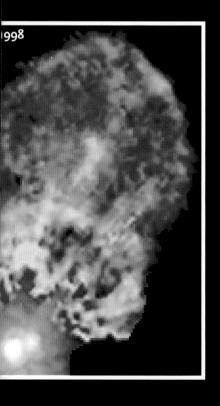

1998

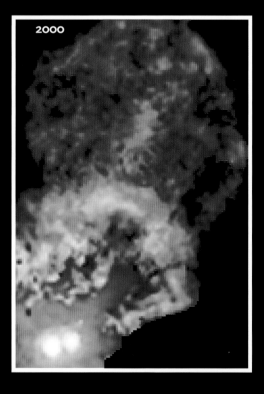

2000

A young binary star system called
XZ Tauri (left) ejects a massive
cloud of hot gas, in a series of
images taken over a period of
five years by the Hubble Space
Telescope. The gas, which began
erupting from the stars about 30
years ago, extends nearly 60
billion miles (96 billion
kilometers) into space.
Astronomers were unsure why
the stars are releasing such a
large amount of gas.

HOW OLD ARE THE STARS?

Stars, like people, have life cycles. Stars pass through stages comparable to infancy, youth, maturity, and old age. Stars eventually die. The life span of a star depends on its **mass** (amount of matter).

A LIFE SPAN IN THE MIDDLE

The sun is an intermediate-mass star. Such stars may last for tens of billions of years. At present, the sun has plenty of fuel to sustain **nuclear fusion** and produce light and heat.

FOLLOWING THE LIGHT

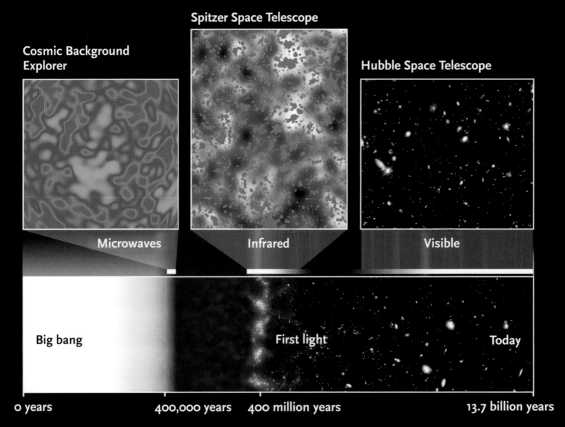

Spitzer Space Telescope

Cosmic Background Explorer

Hubble Space Telescope

Microwaves | Infrared | Visible

Big bang | First light | Today

0 years | 400,000 years | 400 million years | 13.7 billion years

The oldest *photons* (light particles), produced by the big bang, are still moving through space as the cosmic microwave background radiation.

The Spitzer Space Telescope has captured images of some of the first light ever produced by stars.

The Hubble Space Telescope has captured images of some of the earliest galaxies formed in the universe.

Astronomers estimate that the sun will continue to shine for about another 5 billion years.

When all the **hydrogen** in the sun finally *fuses* (combines) to produce **helium, gravity** will pull more matter down into the **core.** This compression will heat the core and surrounding area to such high temperatures that hydrogen fusion will begin in a thin shell surrounding the core. This fusion will push against the sun's outer layers, causing them to expand enormously. As the outer layers cool, the sun will become redder. As the sun's surface area expands greatly, the sun will become brighter. The sun will become a type of star known as a **red giant.** As the sun expands, it will destroy Mercury, Venus, and possibly Earth. Finally, it will shrink and become a **white dwarf** star. The white dwarf will eventually cool to become a **black dwarf.**

AT THE HIGH END

High-mass stars form quickly and have short lives. They may last for only several million years. After their hydrogen is fused to helium, they collapse into a tiny ball and then explode violently. Such an event, called a **supernova**, can be billions of times as bright as the sun before gradually fading from view.

AT THE LOW END

Low-mass stars use hydrogen fuel so slowly that they may shine for tens of billions, possibly even trillions of years. This expected life span is longer than the present age of the universe, believed to be about 13.7 billion years. Therefore, scientists believe no low-mass star has ever died by running out of fuel.

A gamma-ray burst (GRB) flares in an image taken by the Hubble Space Telescope. Astronomers believe that GRB's, which last only a few seconds, are extremely energetic events caused by the explosions of supermassive stars. Astronomers believe that many of these stars, which were more massive than any existing stars, formed very early in the history of the universe.

ANCIENT NAMES

Since the beginning of history, people have recognized pictures or patterns called **constellations** among particular groups of stars. Such patterns have helped people identify stars in the night sky.

Stargazers in the Northern Hemisphere can easily see the Big Dipper, part of the constellation Ursa Major. This group of stars looks somewhat like a *ladle* (a drinking cup with a long handle). Stargazers in the Southern Hemisphere can easily identify the constellation known as the Southern Cross. Its bright stars form a shape that resembles a cross. These star groupings have no meaning in and of themselves. The stars within a constellation are actually quite distant from each other. To us, they appear close together because their light comes from the same region of the sky.

MODERN CONSTELLATIONS

Modern astronomers also use constellations to locate stars in the sky. The International Astronomical Union (IAU), the world authority for assigning names to celestial objects, officially recognizes 88 constellations. These constellations are scattered through the sky. In most cases, the brightest star in a given constellation has *alpha*—the first letter of the

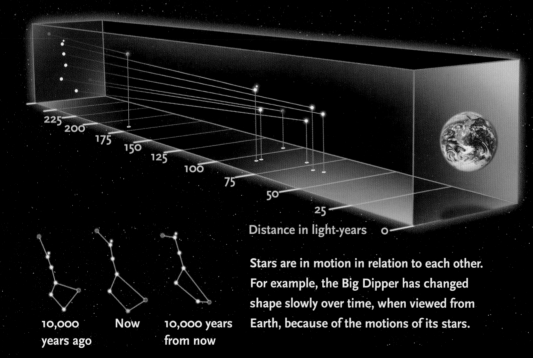

225 200 175 150 125 100 75 50 25

Distance in light-years   0

10,000 years ago   Now   10,000 years from now

Stars are in motion in relation to each other. For example, the Big Dipper has changed shape slowly over time, when viewed from Earth, because of the motions of its stars.

The stars that make up a constellation appear to be the same distance from Earth, but they are not. The stars in the Big Dipper range from about 60 to about 210 light-years from Earth. They appear to be the same distance because they are all so far away and appear in the same area of the sky.

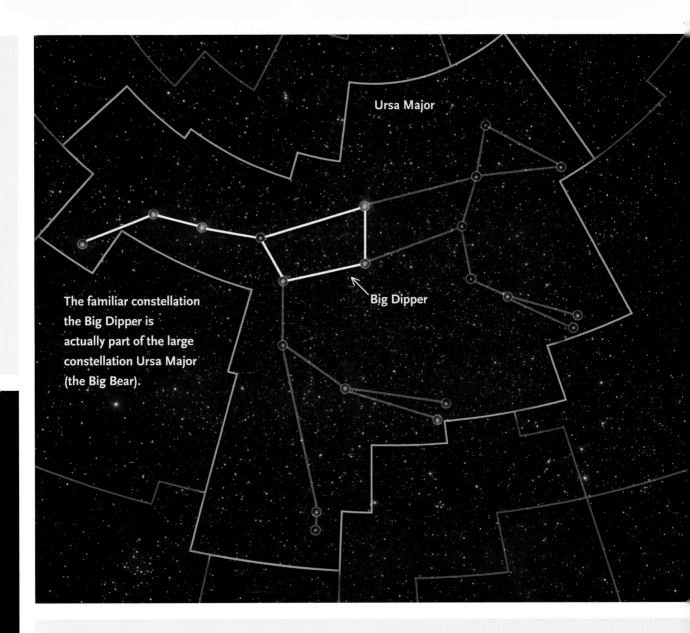

Ursa Major

Big Dipper

The familiar constellation the Big Dipper is actually part of the large constellation Ursa Major (the Big Bear).

Greek alphabet—as part of its scientific name. For instance, the scientific name for Vega, the brightest star in the constellation Lyra (the Harp), is Alpha Lyrae. Lyrae is Latin for *of Lyra*.

The number of known stars has become so large that the IAU uses a different system for newly discovered stars. Most names for these stars consist of an abbreviation followed by a group of symbols. The abbreviation stands for either the type of star or a catalog that lists information about the star. The symbols indicate the star's location in the sky.

WHY DO CONSTELLATIONS CHANGE WITH LATITUDE AND SEASON?

The night sky can appear very different to a stargazer on Earth depending on the time of year and the stargazer's position on the globe.

Like the sun and moon, **constellations** seem to rise and set daily along Earth's horizon. In reality, Earth's *rotation* (spinning motion) causes these effects. However, other changes we see in constellations depend upon **latitude** and season.

LATITUDE

Latitude describes a location on Earth's surface relative to the equator—that is, the distance north or south of this imaginary line. People in Canada, a country in the Northern Hemisphere,

How we see constellations depends on our position on Earth. Our angle of view changes with the four seasons, as Earth's axis changes in relation to the sun.

see a different part of the sky than people in New Zealand, which lies in the Southern Hemisphere. People in these countries view the night sky from different angles.

SEASONS

Earth's seasons are caused by a tilt in Earth's axis as it orbits the sun. The axis is an imaginary line that passes through Earth from the North Pole to the South Pole. When our part of Earth is tilted toward the sun, we enjoy summer. Six months later, when our part of the **planet** is tilted away from the sun, we experience winter. This tilt changes the angle at which we view the night sky. That is why some constellations appear in the sky only in certain seasons. For example, people in the northern United States see Orion (the Hunter) as a winter constellation. It seems to climb above the southern horizon in late fall and can be seen best in December and January.

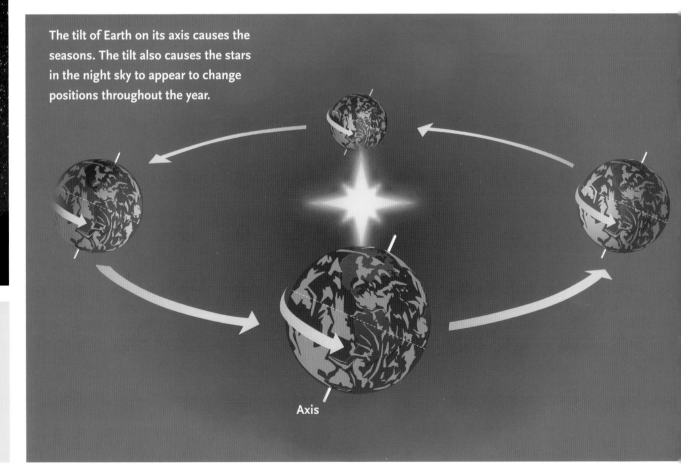

The tilt of Earth on its axis causes the seasons. The tilt also causes the stars in the night sky to appear to change positions throughout the year.

Axis

NEUTRON STARS—
SMALL BUT POWERFUL

The Jellyfish Nebula, formally known as IC 443, is the remains of a star that exploded thousands of years ago. The supernova left behind a neutron star (inset, right).

Neutron stars are the remains of a massive star that exploded in a supernova. They are so dense that one tablespoon of material from a neutron star would weigh as much as 3,000 aircraft carriers. Neutron stars come in several different forms. Some, called pulsars, produce jets of radio waves that sweep across the universe as the star spins. All neutron stars have strong magnetic fields, but some, called magnetars, are thought to be the most magnetized objects in the universe. Some scientists believe that neutron stars can evolve and develop new traits while losing others. For example, one might suddenly stop giving off radio waves and start to give off X rays.

▲ A neutron star can produce powerful jets of energy from two opposite sides (thick white lines, above). It can also be extremely magnetic, producing powerful magnetic fields (thin blue lines). The star in this artist's depiction would probably be classified as a pulsar.

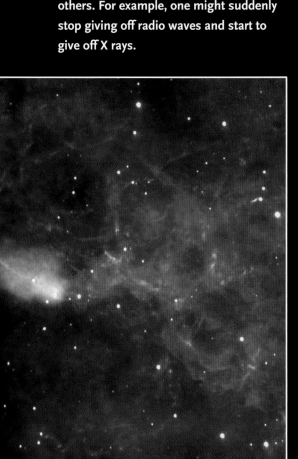

◄ The neutron star in the Jellyfish Nebula (inset, left) is located near the edge of the nebula. This location suggests the explosion that created the nebula and neutron star did not happen equally in every direction. Curiously, the neutron star is not moving away from the center of the cloud but sideways to it.

WHY DO WE SEE STARS ONLY AT NIGHT?

A breathtaking array of stars forms a brilliant canopy over the mountains near Flagstaff, Arizona, the first International Dark Sky City. In 1958, Flagstaff became the first city to limit the use of lights for advertisements. Flagstaff's lighting code protects the city from light pollution, enabling people to enjoy the majesty of the night sky as it appeared before cities flooded the sky with artificial light.

A DAILY TURN

Earth completes one turn on its axis every 24 hours. This rotation causes day and night on Earth. When we see daylight, we are on the side of Earth that is facing the sun. When we see night, we are turned away from the sun, facing outer space.

A MATTER OF DISTANCE

Although there are many **stars** that shine more brightly than the sun, all are so far away that their light has become faint by the time it reaches the **solar system.** During the day, the sun's brilliance blots out these dimmer light beams.

Stars surround Earth in all directions, but during the day, the sun's brightness overwhelms the relatively dim light of other stars.

On summer nights, people often see fireflies twinkling like stars near the ground. If someone turns on a bright floodlight, the fireflies' light is much harder to see. This effect is similar to sunlight's effect on starlight.

CITY LIGHTS

People who live in or near big cities often see stars only faintly at night. That is because many cities in our modern world have grown so large and use so much artificial light at night. Scientists report that in many parts of the eastern United States and Canada, in parts of Europe, and in Japan, city dwellers often can see only a handful of the brightest stars, even on a clear, moonless night. The effect of bright city lights on starlight is similar to that of sunlight. City lights blot out the faint light of most stars. This excess light is called **light pollution.**

Heavily populated areas of Earth glow with artificial light in a map produced with data from United States orbiting satellites. Illumination from streetlights and other artificial light sources "leaks" into the sky, causing light pollution. This pollution severely limits the number of stars visible in the night sky.

WHY DO STARS TWINKLE?

ATMOSPHERIC ILLUSION

In the night sky, **stars** seem to wink in and out continually. The twinkling of stars, however, is a trick of Earth's atmosphere. Astronauts working on the International Space Station see steady, unchanging light from the stars. That is because there is no atmosphere in space to disturb the rays of light coming from the stars.

Light travels in straight lines unless it is disturbed. Earth's atmosphere has many layers, and there is much movement of air, dust, and water vapor in most of these layers. These particles in motion disturb stars' faint light beams passing through the atmosphere.

In order to overcome the distortion caused by the atmosphere, astronomers have developed a technique called **adaptive optics.**

TWINKLE-LESS STARGAZING

Because of its position outside Earth's atmosphere, the Hubble Space Telescope can view stars without interference. The images of stars created by Hubble are clearer and more detailed than any images seen by telescopes on Earth.

A laser beam aimed into the sky helps astronomers at the Keck Observatory on Mauna Kea, Hawaii, map the distortion of light caused by the atmosphere. Sensors on the telescope can measure the effect the atmosphere has over the entire length of the laser beam. Astronomers use this information as part of a system called adaptive optics to help focus the telescope in a way that eliminates the distortion.

DID YOU KNOW?

Hydra (the Water Serpent) is the largest constellation in area. The smallest constellation is the Southern Cross, also known as Crux.

Stars do not really twinkle. They appear to twinkle because pockets of moving air bend starlight as it passes through Earth's dense atmosphere.

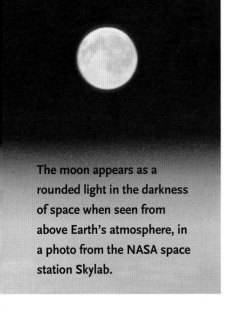

The moon appears as a rounded light in the darkness of space when seen from above Earth's atmosphere, in a photo from the NASA space station Skylab.

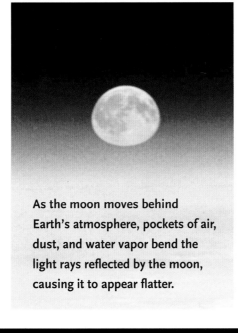

As the moon moves behind Earth's atmosphere, pockets of air, dust, and water vapor bend the light rays reflected by the moon, causing it to appear flatter.

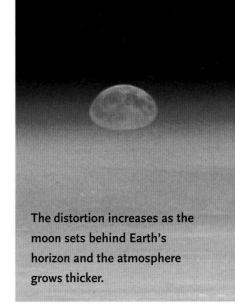

The distortion increases as the moon sets behind Earth's horizon and the atmosphere grows thicker.

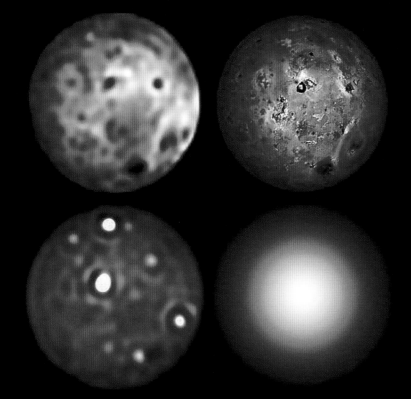

Adaptive optics enables astronomers to correct for the blurring effects of Earth's atmosphere. Jupiter's moon Io appears in much greater detail in images taken by the Keck Telescope using adaptive optics (far left, top and bottom) than in an image made without the technology (left, bottom). The images made using adaptive optics almost rival an image of Io taken by the Jupiter probe Galileo from a much closer distance (left, top).

HOW BIG ARE STARS?

The star Eta Carinae is a massive star that scientists believe is close to exploding in a supernova. The star is ejecting huge amounts of gas (colorized in blue) into space.

UNIVERSAL HEAVYWEIGHTS

Stars are large compared with the **planets** in the **solar system,** even Jupiter, the largest planet. The sun is about 10 times as wide as Jupiter, but it is actually classified as a "yellow dwarf" by astronomers. Many stars are much larger than the sun. Some stars are called "supergiants" because of their huge size. Some collapsed stars, on the other hand, are considerably smaller than Earth.

Astronomers measure the size of stars in comparison to the sun's radius. (A radius is the distance from the center of a sphere or circle to the outside. The plural of *radius* is *radii*.) The largest **red supergiants** are about 1,500 solar radii. In other words, the radius of one of these stars is 1,500 times that of the sun.

DID YOU KNOW?

The star Arcturus provided the lighting for the opening night of Chicago's 1933 world's fair, called "A Century of Progress." Telescopes captured the star's light rays on photoelectric cells, which generated enough electric power to turn on the lights.

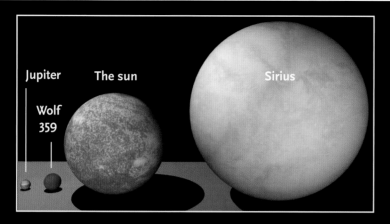

The planet Jupiter and the red dwarf Wolf 359 are much smaller than the sun and Sirius, the brightest star in Earth's night sky.

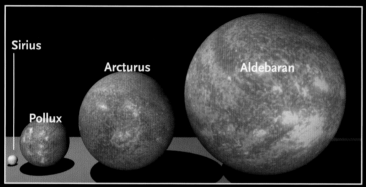

Sirius is quite small compared with stars designated as giants—including Pollux—and as supergiants—including Arcturus and Aldebaran.

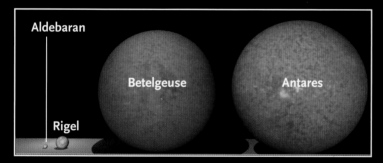

Although Aldebaran and Antares are both classified as supergiants, their size difference is considerable.

The largest stars known, including S Doradus and VV Cephei, are sometimes referred to as "hypergiants." These stars are rare and shine for only about 1 million years. In contrast, the sun will shine for 10 billion years.

WHY DO STARS SHINE?

FROM MASS TO LIGHT

Most **stars** are made of gases and a form of matter called **plasma.** Plasma is similar to a gas in many ways, such as its ability to flow. However, plasma is so hot that its atoms have come apart, leaving such electrically charged particles as nuclei and electrons. In stars, plasma can reach temperatures of millions of degrees. The incredibly high pressure and hot temperatures in the interiors of stars cause the *nuclei* (cores) of the atoms there to *fuse* (combine). This process is called **nuclear fusion.** When two nuclei fuse, a small amount of their **mass** turns to energy. Some of this energy is *emitted* (sent out) as **visible light.** Within most stars, including the sun, nuclear fusion occurs constantly. This process produces a steady stream of visible light and other forms of **electromagnetic radiation.**

THE LIGHT WE NEED

Visible light is one of seven *bands* (types) of electromagnetic radiation emitted by stars. Most of the energy emitted by the sun is visible light and **infrared rays,** which we feel as heat. Like infrared rays, the remaining energy emitted by the sun is invisible to human eyes. This energy consists of **radio waves, microwaves, ultraviolet light, X rays,** and **gamma rays**. (The form of energy known as microwaves is considered a type of radio wave.) The amount of energy in electromagnetic waves is directly related to

DID YOU KNOW?

Some stars are actually green—and purple. We don't see those colors, though, because those stars are so far away that our eyes can't detect the green and purple bands of the color spectrum as well as they can the other colors.

Most of the energy *emitted* (given off) by the sun consists of visible light and of another form of radiation called infrared light, which we feel as heat. However, the sun emits radiation of each type in the electromagnetic spectrum.

their **wavelength**—that is, the distance between the *crest* (high point) of one wave and the next. The more energetic the radiation, the shorter is the wavelength. For example, gamma rays have shorter wavelengths than radio waves. For this reason, gamma rays have more energy than radio waves.

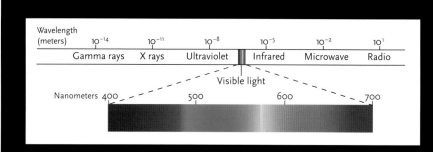

Wavelength (meters)	10^{-14}	10^{-11}	10^{-8}	10^{-5}	10^{-2}	10^{1}
	Gamma rays	X rays	Ultraviolet	Infrared	Microwave	Radio

Visible light

Nanometers 400   500   600   700

The electromagnetic spectrum is commonly separated into seven sections ranging from gamma rays to radio wave

A hydrogen bomb uses the fusion of hydrogen to produce tremendous energy.

WHAT IS VISIBLE LIGHT?

A rare type of rainbow called a circumhorizontal arc appears in the sky above Ohio. The rainbow occurs when ice crystals high in the atmosphere act like prisms, breaking the light into various colors.

FROM RAYS TO PARTICLES

People once thought **visible light** was something that traveled from a person's eyes to an object and then back again. Ancient scholars pictured light as traveling in rays. We now understand that visible light is one form of **electromagnetic radiation.** This energy travels freely through space in patterns of electric and magnetic force that take the form of waves. Human beings can see only a tiny part of the electromagnetic **spectrum** (bands of energy). Electromagnetic radiation invisible to human eyes includes **radio waves, ultraviolet light,** and **X rays.** These different forms of light can be distinguished by their **wavelength** and energy. Wavelength is the distance between the *crest* (high point) of one wave and the next.

Although light has properties of a wave, scientists have demonstrated that light is also made up of extremely tiny particles called **photons.** Unlike other particles, photons have no **mass** (amount of matter). They also have no electric charge. In a vacuum, photons travel at the speed of light—about 186,282 miles (299,792 kilometers) per second. Nothing in the universe can travel faster.

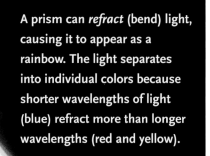

A prism can *refract* (bend) light, causing it to appear as a rainbow. The light separates into individual colors because shorter wavelengths of light (blue) refract more than longer wavelengths (red and yellow).

LIGHT OF A DIFFERENT COLOR

Visible light includes bands of violet, blue, green, yellow, orange, and red, and many shades between. Light appears to be white when we see all the colors of the spectrum at the same time. A spectrum is a band of light arranged in order of wavelength. The collection of colors we can see makes up the visible spectrum.

Individual colors can be separated using a **prism,** a specially shaped piece of glass or other clear material that bends light rays. In the sky, a rainbow appears when raindrops act as prisms to separate out the colors of light.

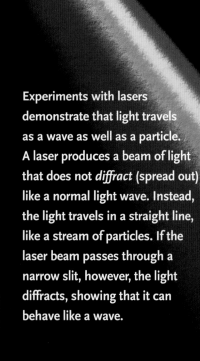

Experiments with lasers demonstrate that light travels as a wave as well as a particle. A laser produces a beam of light that does not *diffract* (spread out) like a normal light wave. Instead, the light travels in a straight line, like a stream of particles. If the laser beam passes through a narrow slit, however, the light diffracts, showing that it can behave like a wave.

WHAT IS A STAR LIKE ON THE INSIDE?

PLASMA

Temperatures within a **star** are so extreme that none of its matter can exist in either solid or liquid form. All of the matter inside a star is either a gas or a gas-like substance called **plasma.** Plasma is so hot that its atoms have come apart, leaving such electrically charged particles as nuclei and electrons.

Like the sun, other stars consist mainly of the **chemical element hydrogen,** with some **helium** and small amounts of other elements. **Nuclear fusion** reactions take place in the **core** (central area) of a star. There, hydrogen *fuses* (combines) into helium, producing great amounts of energy.

INSIDE TO OUTSIDE

The sun has several zones, or layers. We cannot see the sun's core, but scientists have studied it

A sun-like star consists of many layers. The temperatures in the innermost layers, where nuclear fusion occurs, reach millions of degrees. The photosphere produces the light we see. In addition, sunspots appear in this layer. Large features, including solar flares and prominences, can be seen in the corona. These features can affect weather and electric power on Earth.

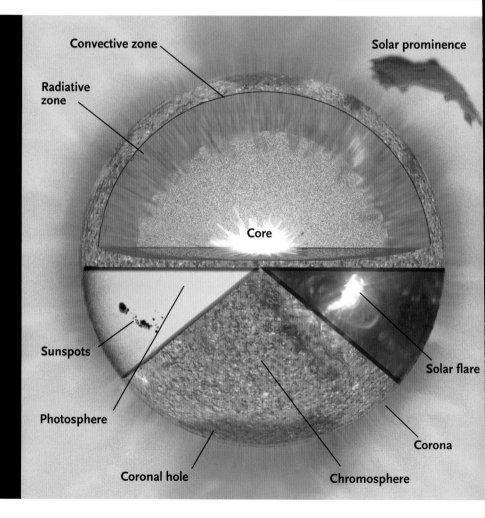

Convective zone

Solar prominence

Radiative zone

Core

Sunspots

Photosphere

Solar flare

Corona

Coronal hole

Chromosphere

In a "plasma ball," electricity is used to create a magnetic field inside the ball. The field causes an *inert* (nonreactive) gas to become a plasma, the gas-like matter in stars.

indirectly by analyzing measurements taken of the sun as a whole. The core is by far the densest, hottest zone. Scientists estimate that it is about twice as dense as lead and has a temperature of many millions of degrees. Moving outward from the core, the next zone is the radiative zone. Light and other forms of energy pass through this dense, hot region.

The next layer, the convection zone, extends to the sun's surface. The surface of the sun is much cooler than the core. Beyond the convection zone is the sun's atmosphere. The sun's atmosphere is much hotter than the convection zone. Scientists still debate the reason for this oddness, though it may involve the sun's **magnetic fields.**

Stars are not all alike. Some giant stars have more complex interiors than the sun, including more layers and a more complex surface. Scientists are just beginning to understand how these giant stars are different from the sun and how they evolve.

HOW DO STARS MAKE CHEMICAL ELEMENTS?

BEGINNING WITH THE BASICS

A **chemical element** is a substance consisting of only one kind of atom. An atom is the smallest particle of matter that can exist under normal conditions of temperature and pressure. Elements are the building blocks of matter in the universe. The element with the simplest atomic structure is **hydrogen.** It has one *proton* (positively charged particle) in its *nucleus* (core) with one *electron* (negatively charged particle) bound to it. Because hydrogen has only one proton, it has the smallest **mass** (amount of matter) of any chemical element.

In the early universe, most matter consisted of hydrogen gas. Then stars began to form. Inside the stars, **nuclear fusion** took place. The hydrogen began *fusing* (combining) into a slightly heavier element, **helium.** After millions of years, the hydrogen began to run out, and helium began fusing to form even heavier elements. This transition from mostly hydrogen to mostly helium occurs over time in all stars.

A supernova remnant rich in iron (above, left) appears to be colliding with another remnant with much less of the chemical element in the Large Magellanic Cloud galaxy. Most of the heavier chemical elements found in the universe, including gold and uranium, are created during such stellar explosions.

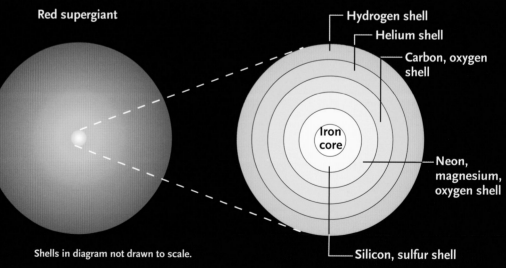

A huge star creates chemical elements by nuclear fusion, the joining of two atomic nuclei to make a larger nucleus. In the outermost shell, hydrogen nuclei fuse, creating helium. In the next shell, helium fuses to make carbon and oxygen. Fusion creates successively heavier elements in shells closer to the core, where iron is produced.

Red supergiant

Hydrogen shell
Helium shell
Carbon, oxygen shell
Iron core
Neon, magnesium, oxygen shell
Silicon, sulfur shell

Shells in diagram not drawn to scale.

Chemical elements are produced by the combination of atomic particles in a star's core. Violently exploding giant stars called supernovae create the heavier elements.

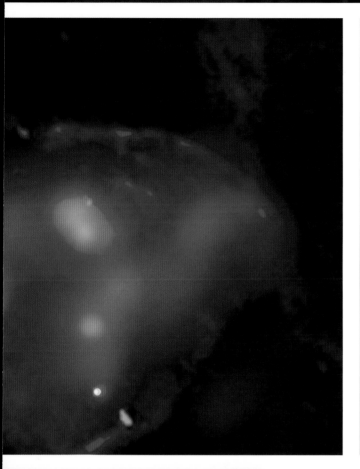

When a star explodes as a supernova, heavy chemical elements are blasted into space. The shock waves generated by the supernova can trigger the birth of new stars in the clouds of dust and gas with these elements.

With each heavier element, the star runs through its fuel more quickly. A red supergiant with 25 times as much mass as the sun might fuse helium for about 700,000 years; carbon for 1,000 years; neon for 9 months; oxygen for 4 months; and silicon for about 1 day. When all the silicon in the star's core has been fused to iron, the star is doomed. Fusion of iron consumes energy instead of releasing it, and the star collapses inward.

FACTORIES FOR THE ELEMENTS

As stars age, they begin to fuse heavier and heavier elements. After a very long time, a star begins fusing helium to create such elements as carbon, oxygen, neon, and silicon. Supergiant stars are factories for the production of still-heavier elements, including gold, lead, and mercury. That is because at the end of its life, a supergiant star explodes with tremendous violence as a **supernova.** This explosion creates heavy elements and shoots them into space. Supernova explosions enrich the interstellar gas clouds that eventually form stars and planets. Most of the elements that make up our planet originated in supernova explosions.

A TURBULENT SURFACE

The surface of a **star** such as the sun is not smooth and calm. Disturbances of various kinds occur. One of these disturbances is a sunspot, a relatively dark area with a very strong **magnetic field.** Sunspots appear dark because they are cooler than the rest of the sun's visible surface. The magnetic fields in sunspots are up to 3,000 times as strong as the average magnetic field of either the sun or Earth.

THE ATMOSPHERE OF A SUN-LIKE STAR

A sun-like star also has an atmosphere, a layer that extends from its surface to the outer edge. The atmosphere of a sun-like star is very active and often violent.

The lowest layer of the sun's atmosphere is called the photosphere. The sun's photosphere sends out the sunlight we see on Earth. Above the photosphere is the chromosphere. This atmospheric layer is much hotter than the underlying photosphere. The upper layer of the sun's atmosphere is called the corona. The corona is the hottest atmospheric layer. It is so hot that it continually expands outward into space, throwing off energetic particles. This flow of coronal gas into space is known as the **solar wind.**

STORMS FROM THE SUN

Several types of storms take place in the atmosphere of a sun-like star. Among these storms are flares, coronal loops, and coronal mass ejections (CME's). CME's are balls of electrically charged **plasma** blasted outward from the corona. They have the energy of a billion hydrogen bombs. These solar storms can

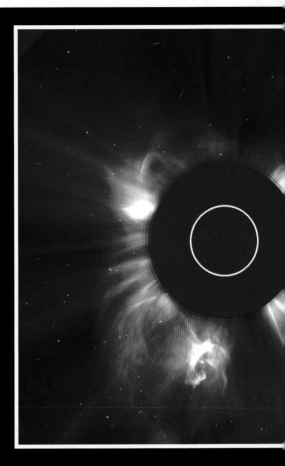

A large group of sunspots covers an area 13 times the surface area of Earth. Sunspots appear darker because they are relatively cooler than the visible surface of the sun.

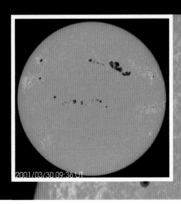

2001/03/30 09:36 UT

The surface and atmosphere of such stars as the sun are very active. They have changeable features, including sunspots and solar flares.

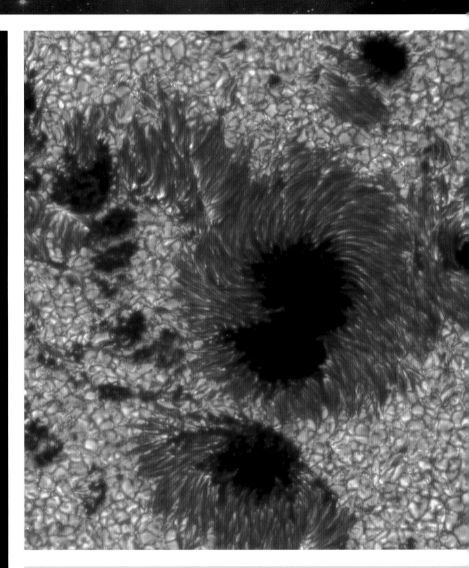

Electrically charged particles blast into space from the sun at millions of miles per hour (left) during a "storm" called a coronal mass ejection. The light from the central part of the sun is blocked in the image by a device called a coronagraph, which allows astronomers to view a star's outer layers in great detail.

Sunspots (right) are disturbances in the surface of the sun thought to be associated with the sun's magnetic field.

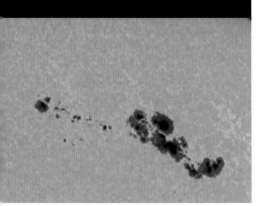

interfere with or severely damage Earth-orbiting satellites as well as power and communication systems on Earth.

Stars that have a **mass** similar to that of the sun likely experience similar disturbances. Smaller stars will generally have less active atmospheres, while larger stars experience atmospheric disturbances far more violent than those of the sun.

SUPERNOVAE—BLASTS FROM THE PAST

A supernova is an exploding star. It can become billions of times as bright as the sun before fading from view. At its brightest, a supernova may outshine an entire galaxy. The explosion throws a large cloud of gas into space at huge speeds. The mass of the expelled material may exceed 10 times the sun's mass. Most supernovae reach their peak brightness in one to three weeks and shine intensely for several months. Scientists believe heavy elements, such as gold and uranium, are made in supernovae. Scientists can also learn about the evolution of stars from observing supernovae.

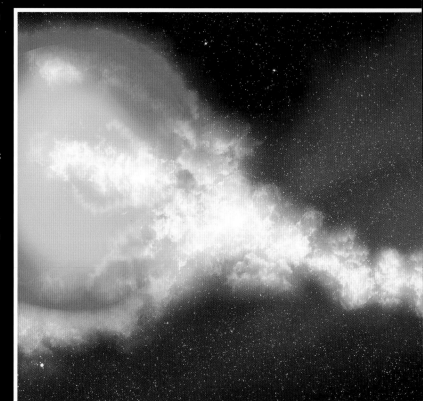

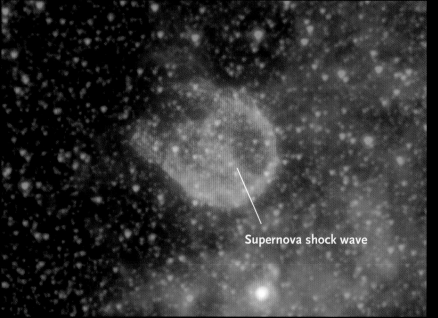

Supernova shock wave

A cloud of hot gas, shown as a pink shell (left) in a false-color image from the Chandra X-ray Observatory, is the remains of a Type II supernova, or core-collapse supernova. Such supernovae occur when the core of a supermassive star runs out of fuel and collapses. The sudden release of energy from the collapsed core causes the star to explode.

Type Ia supernovae, also called thermonuclear supernovae, occur in certain *binary* (double) star systems that include a small dense star called a white dwarf. If the stars are close enough, the gravitational pull of the white dwarf slowly strips material from its companion star, as shown (left) in an artist's illustration. Over time, matter builds up in the white dwarf, causing a massive fusion reaction in its core. This reaction causes the release of a huge amount of energy that causes the white dwarf to explode in a supernova.

Scientists believe that the Tycho supernova remnant (right) is the remains of a Type Ia supernova that occurred in 1572. The remnant is named for Danish astronomer Tycho Brahe, who observed and described it. The supernova was so bright it was visible in daylight for more than two weeks. This image combines photographs taken by the Chandra X-ray Observatory, the Spitzer Space Telescope, and the Calar Alto Observatory in Spain.

HOW BRIGHT ARE STARS?

BRIGHT AND BRIGHTER

Anyone who gazes into the night sky immediately notices that some stars are brighter than others. Many are very faint. A few seem very bright. The scientific term that describes the brightness of stars is **magnitude.** When describing stars as seen from Earth in the night sky, scientists use the term *apparent magnitude. Apparent* means *seeming* or *appearing as.*

A MATTER OF ENERGY AND DISTANCE

How bright a star looks when viewed from Earth depends on two factors. The first is the actual brightness of the star—that is, the amount of light energy the star *emits* (sends out). The second is the distance from Earth to the star. A nearby star that is dim can appear brighter than a distant star that is extremely brilliant. For example, Alpha Centauri A seems to be slightly brighter than a star known as Rigel. But Alpha Centauri A emits only 1/100,000 as much light

DID YOU KNOW?

A star with a magnitude of 0.0 is about 2.5 times as bright as a star with a magnitude of 1.0.

The Serpens South star cluster is one of many collections of young, bright stars held together by gravity.

Sirius A, also known as the Dog Star, is the brightest star in Earth's night sky. It gives off nearly 30 times as much light as the sun.

energy as Rigel. Alpha Centauri A seems brighter because it is only about 1/200 as far from Earth as Rigel is—4.4 **light-years** for Alpha Centauri A, compared with 700-900 light-years for Rigel.

In ancient times, some observers thought the night sky was a hollow sphere around Earth and that the stars were embedded in this sphere like lights in a ceiling. Later astronomers came to realize that there was no such structure in the sky and that the distance of stars from Earth varies greatly. The brightness of stars as viewed from Earth is not the same as their brightness if viewed from other places in the universe. As a result, scientists began referring to the brightness of stars as they appear from Earth as apparent magnitude.

The 10 brightest stars as seen from Earth

Common name	Scientific name	Distance (light-years)	Apparent magnitude	Absolute magnitude	Spectral type
1. Sun		0.00001	−26.72	4.8	G2V
2. Sirius*	Alpha Canis Majoris	8.6	21.46	1.4	A1V 1 WD†
3. Canopus	Alpha Carinae	313	20.72	22.5	F0Ib
4. Rigel Kentaurus	*Alpha Centauri	4.4	20.27	4.4	G2V 1 K1V
5. Arcturus	Alpha Boötis	37	20.04	0.2	K2III
6. Vega	Alpha Lyrae	25	0.03	0.6	A0V
7. Capella*	Alpha Aurigae	42	0.08	-0.4	G6III 1 G2III
8. Rigel‡	Beta Orionis	700-900§	0.12	28.1	B8Ia
9. Procyon*	Alpha Canis Minoris	11.5	0.38	2.6	F5IV + WD†
10. Achernar	Alpha Eridani	144	0.46	21.3	B3V

* Binary star system.   † White dwarf.   ‡ Triple star system.   § Estimate.

ARE STARS AS BRIGHT AS THEY LOOK?

WHAT YOU SEE

The term apparent **magnitude** describes the brightness of stars as seen from Earth. But that is not the whole story. From Earth, the sun appears incredibly bright. That is because it is relatively close to our planet—not because it is an especially bright star. Distance is a major factor in the apparent brightness of a star. Another factor is **luminosity,** the rate at which a star *emits* (gives off) light and other forms of energy.

WHAT YOU GET

To consider the brightness of a star apart from its distance, astronomers use the term *absolute magnitude*. Absolute magnitude depends upon luminosity. To determine absolute magnitude, astronomers calculate the brightness of stars as if they were all the same distance from Earth— 32.6 **light-years**.

MEASURING ABSOLUTE MAGNITUDE

In the number scale that astronomers use for the absolute magnitude of stars, the brighter a star or planet, the lower its magnitude number. The brightest star in the night sky is Sirius, with an absolute magnitude of −1.45. The sun has an absolute magnitude of 4.8, which indicates that it is less luminous than Sirius. Large ground-based telescopes can detect stars with an absolute magnitude of 25. The magnitude system is based on the work of the ancient Greek astronomer Hipparchus in about 125 B.C.

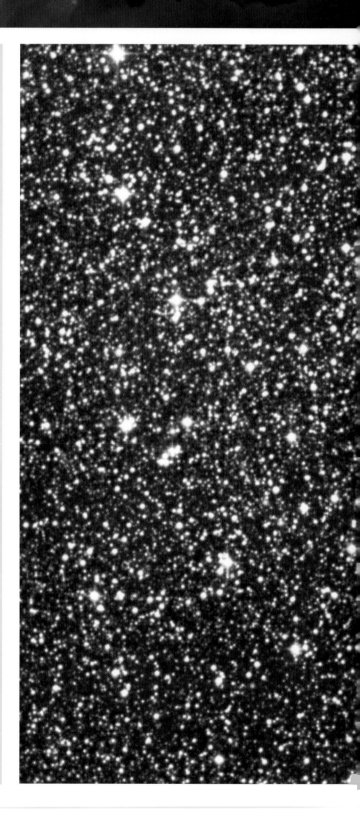

Proxima Centauri (arrow, below) is the closest star to the sun, at 4.22 light-years away. Much smaller than the sun, it is 10,000 times as faint. Because of its dimness, it can only be seen with a telescope.

The ancient Greek astronomer Hipparchus classified the stars based on their brightness in about 125 B.C. His work served as the basis for the magnitude scale used by modern astronomers, which measures a star's brightness as seen from Earth.

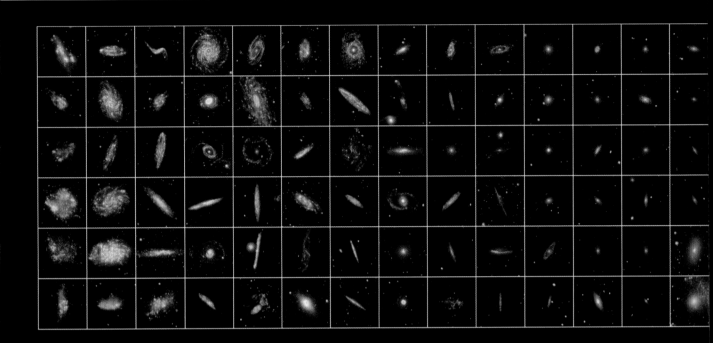

The age of a galaxy can be estimated by its color. Young stars tend to be relatively hot, making them appear blue (left side of chart, above). Older stars tend to cool and shift toward a redder color (right side of chart).

A DIFFERENT SCALE

To express the very high temperatures in stars and other parts of the universe, scientists use the **Kelvin** scale. On the Kelvin scale, zero Kelvin (0 K) represents absolute zero. Absolute zero theoretically is the lowest possible temperature in the universe, −459.67 °F (−273.15 °C). (The word *degree* and the degree symbol [°] are not used with Kelvin temperature readings.) On the Kelvin scale, each degree of heat is measured in the same unit as in the metric Celsius system. So, in Kelvin, the melting point of ice is 273.15 K (the same as 0 °C).

DID YOU KNOW?

The inner core of Earth may be hotter than the surface of the sun.

Although all stars are very hot, they vary in temperature, especially in surface temperature. The cores of stars, where nuclear fusion takes place, are the hottest parts of stars.

The surface temperature of a **red giant star** ranges from about 2,500 to 3,500 K, and the surface temperature of a yellow dwarf, such as the sun, is about 5,500 K. Blue stars have a much hotter surface than either of these. The surface temperature of a blue star can range as high as 50,000 K. The core of the sun is more than 15 million K. That figure equals about 27 million °F (15 million °C).

HOW HOT CAN HOT GET?

Absolute zero is the coldest possible temperature, but is there any absolute maximum for extremely hot temperatures? Scientists say that theoretically, there is no upper limit for temperature. Some stars, for example, may have cores as hot as 200 million K. Scientists estimate that **supernovae** may heat up to more than 1 billion K before exploding violently.

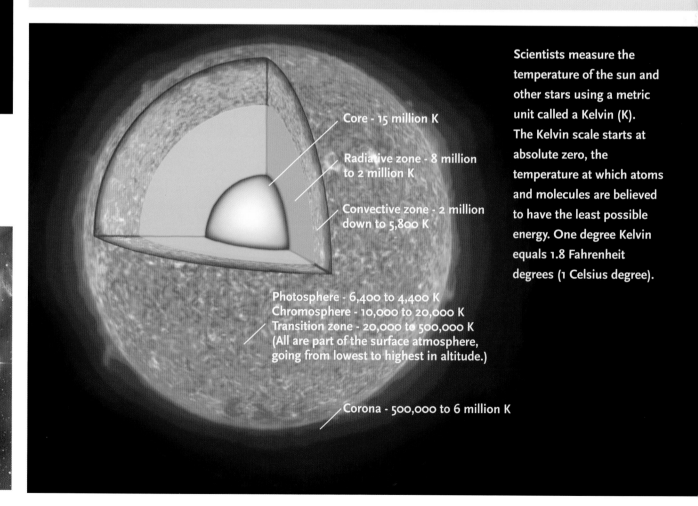

Core - 15 million K

Radiative zone - 8 million to 2 million K

Convective zone - 2 million down to 5,800 K

Photosphere - 6,400 to 4,400 K
Chromosphere - 10,000 to 20,000 K
Transition zone - 20,000 to 500,000 K
(All are part of the surface atmosphere, going from lowest to highest in altitude.)

Corona - 500,000 to 6 million K

Scientists measure the temperature of the sun and other stars using a metric unit called a Kelvin (K). The Kelvin scale starts at absolute zero, the temperature at which atoms and molecules are believed to have the least possible energy. One degree Kelvin equals 1.8 Fahrenheit degrees (1 Celsius degree).

WHY ARE STARS DIFFERENT COLORS?

NOT JUST WHITE

On a clear, moonless night, the sky is ablaze with thousands of **stars**. The casual observer sees a splattering of white on black, but the careful observer begins to see something else: color. Stars emit light of a characteristic color, based upon their surface temperature.

Dark red stars have surface temperatures of about 2,500 K (4,000 °F). The surface temperature of a bright red star is approximately 3,500 K (5,800 °F), and that of the sun and other yellow stars, roughly 5,500 K (9,400 °F). Blue stars range from about 10,000 to 50,000 K (17,500 to 89,500 °F) in surface temperature.

Although a star appears as a single color to the unaided eye, it actually emits a broad **spectrum** (band) of colors. You can see that starlight consists of many colors by using a **prism** to separate and spread the colors of the light of the sun, a yellow star. The visible spectrum includes all the colors of the rainbow. These colors range from red, which has the longest **wavelength,** to violet, which has the shortest.

The crowded core of the Omega Centauri star cluster contains stars of varying colors. The majority of the stars are of a yellow or orange hue, indicating a star in the middle of its life cycle. The red stars are most likely older stars nearing the end of their lives. The youngest stars appear blue and are the hottest stars in the cluster.

Stars shine in different colors, depending on their surface temperature.

FROM YELLOW DWARF TO RED GIANT

Stars do not remain the same forever. As they age, they change. Late in life, the sun will begin to run out of **hydrogen** fuel. It will expand greatly, becoming a **red giant.** This color change is caused by a change in surface temperature. Small stars give off lots of energy because they have a relatively small surface area. As a dying star expands, it may radiate the same amount of energy. However, that radiation covers a much larger surface area. This causes the surface to cool. As it does, the color of the radiated light changes from yellow to red.

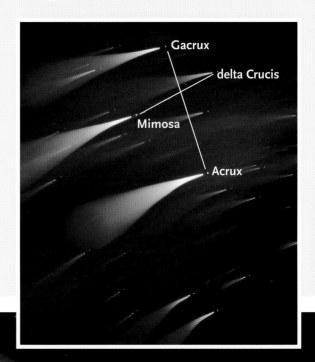

The actual colors of the stars that make up the Southern Cross constellation (above), also known as Crux, stand out in a time-lapse photograph.

A lingering glow in the layers of dust surrounding a dust cloud, known as a light echo, speeds outward from the red giant V838 Monocerotis after the star suddenly brightened and then dimmed in 2002.

STAR STORIES FROM ANCIENT TIMES

THE GREAT SKY HUNTER

Ancient peoples developed a rich body of *myths* (stories) about their gods and goddesses. Many of these myths involved **constellations.** To the Greeks, the spectacular constellation that rises from the southern horizon in winter looked like a mighty hunter. The Greeks named this hunter Orion.

On clear nights, stargazers can easily see Orion's body, belt, sword, raised right arm with club, and a bow grasped in his raised left hand. Betelgeuse, a **red supergiant,**

The oldest surviving pictorial record of constellations known to the ancient Greeks and Romans may be that on the Farnese Atlas statue, which dates from A.D. 150. The statue depicts the god Atlas after being sentenced by Zeus to hold up the heavens and Earth. The sphere shows the placement of constellations from about 125 B.C. Some scientists think the constellations are a representation of the long-lost star catalog of Hipparchus (180?-125 B.C.?), an ancient Greek astronomer.

The ancient astronomer Ptolemy conducts his observations of the heavens in Alexandria, Egypt, around 100 B.C., in an engraving from the 1800's.

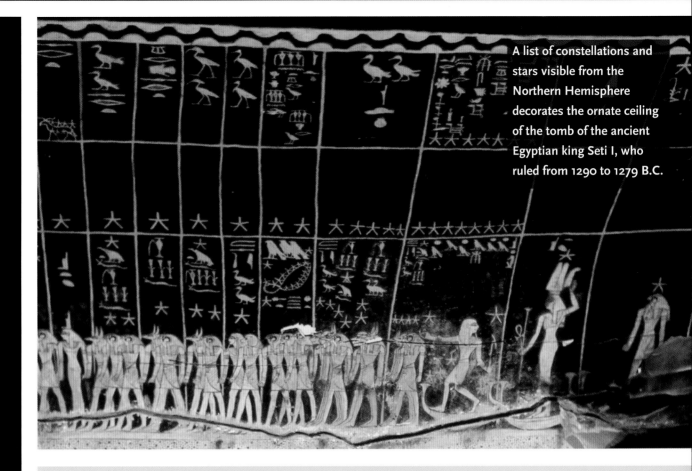

A list of constellations and stars visible from the Northern Hemisphere decorates the ornate ceiling of the tomb of the ancient Egyptian king Seti I, who ruled from 1290 to 1279 B.C.

forms Orion's right shoulder. At Orion's heels is the constellation Canis Major, or "Big Dog," perhaps his faithful hunting dog. The brightest star in the night sky, Sirius, is near the center of Big Dog. Orion seems to be attacking Taurus (the Bull) or chasing the Pleiades, a tight cluster of stars next to the Bull.

Ancient Greek storytellers and writers created a myth about Orion. Orion fell in love with Artemis, the daughter of Zeus, the king of the gods, and the goddess Leto. To win

Artemis, Orion boasted that he could kill every animal on earth. This boast bothered Artemis, because she herself was a great hunter.

Artemis and Leto sent a huge scorpion against Orion, which stung him to death. Zeus rewarded the scorpion by placing it in the heavens. It now can be seen as the constellation Scorpius. To warn people against idle boasting, Zeus also put Orion in the sky. Orion can never let his guard down, because the scorpion dwells with him among the stars.

The Onondaga people lived along the Finger Lakes in what is now New York state, long before settlers came from Holland, England, and other European countries. The Onondaga watched the night skies and created myths about the heavenly bodies. One myth attempts to explain the origin of the Pleiades, a bright group of stars just to the east of the constellations Orion and Taurus in the night sky. Many stargazers think they can see seven stars in the Pleiades, but there are actually many more.

TRAGIC SKY CHILDREN

One year, a band of Onondaga made their autumn camp near a beautiful woodland lake. After the lodges were built and the air became too chilly for swimming, there was little for the Onondaga children to do. So they danced together in a glade by the lake. The children danced hour after hour.

As day faded into night, the children's parents came and begged them to return to their lodges. But the children kept dancing. Presently, an ancient man with hair of shining silver and a cloak of dazzling white feathers appeared to the children. Sternly, he warned them that they must stop dancing, for evil would come to them if they did not.

But the children could not stop dancing. They had danced far too long and too fast, and they were possessed by the dance itself. As the children danced faster and faster, they began to rise into the air. Their parents began to shout in horror to call them back. But it was too late. The dancing children rose all the way up to the heavens. They can now be seen as the seven stars of the Pleiades.

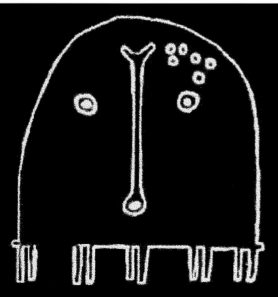

The Flint Boys is the name the Navajo, a Native American tribe, give to the cluster of stars also known as the Pleiades or the Seven Sisters. According to Navajo belief, Black God, the Fire God, came to the first people before the creation of the world. As he entered their meeting place, they noticed he was wearing a cluster of crystals on his ankle. Black God walked around the meeting place and then stamped his foot. The crystals jumped up to his knee. He stamped his foot again, and the crystals jumped to his hip. The first people were pleased that Black God had power over the crystals. Black God then stamped his foot a third time, and the crystals jumped to his shoulder. When he stamped his foot the fourth time, the crystals jumped to his temple. The first people then asked what the crystals were, and Black God told them they were called stars.

An emu engraving (right, bottom) at the Elvina Track Engraving Site in Australia's Kuringai National Park mirrors the Aboriginal emu-in-the-sky constellation superimposed on the Milky Way (right).

STAR STORIES FROM ANCIENT CHINA

China is an ancient culture, and people there have watched the stars for thousands of years. Many years ago, Chinese stargazers developed a myth about the woes of a young couple in love. This myth involves three bright stars that are high in the summer night sky—Altair, Deneb, and Vega. The stars are in or next to the Milky Way, and together they form the three points of a triangle known as "the summer triangle."

A herding-boy was watching his oxen along the banks of a stream. Suddenly, seven celestial maidens descended and bathed in the river. These maidens were all weaver-girls whose job it was to weave clothes for the gods and goddesses in heaven. The herder-boy fell in love at once with the youngest weaver-girl. He persuaded her to stay on Earth and become his wife. The young couple was very happy.

In time, however, the gods and goddesses became angry. The six remaining celestial weaver-girls could not keep up with the gods' and

In Chinese mythology, the weaving maiden and the herding-boy were separated in the night sky by the Milky Way.

DID YOU KNOW?

Our bodies contain the same elements that make up the stars.

goddesses' demands for new clothes. To get revenge, these all-powerful beings transformed the herder-boy into the star Altair in the night sky. They cast the weaver-girl into the sky as the star Vega—and gave her a loom so that she might keep weaving for them. To forever separate husband and wife, they caused a fast-flowing celestial river to flow between these stars. We see this river now as the Milky Way.

The story is not a complete tragedy, however. On one day each year, magpies form a bridge, wing to wing, across the celestial river, allowing the herding-boy to cross for a brief reunion with his beloved. One of these magpies is the star Deneb.

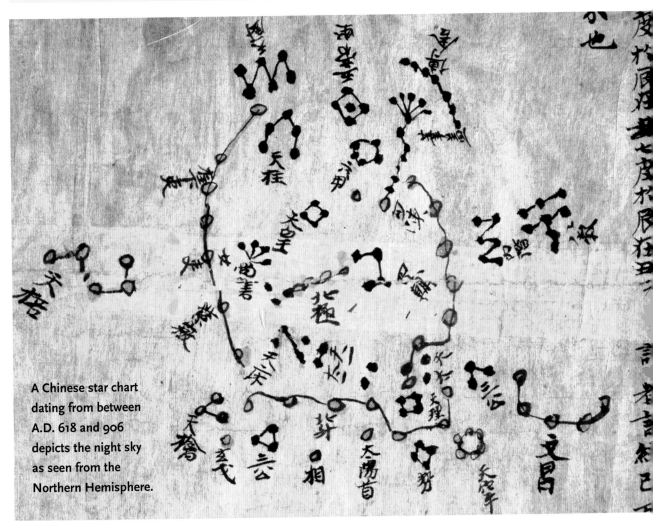

A Chinese star chart dating from between A.D. 618 and 906 depicts the night sky as seen from the Northern Hemisphere.

GLOSSARY

Adaptive optics – A system added to ground-based telescopes to correct for the distorting effects of the atmosphere.

Binary stars – Stars that orbit around each other.

Black dwarf – The dark remnant of a white dwarf that has become too cold to give off light.

Brown dwarf – A failed star that is larger than a planet but smaller than a true star. It cannot sustain nuclear fusion.

Chemical element – Any substance that contains only one kind of atom. Hydrogen and helium are both chemical elements.

Constellation – A group of stars that resembles a familiar shape in the sky. Astronomers have divided the night sky into 88 constellations, such as Orion (the Hunter).

Core – The dense, hot center of a star.

Dwarf star – A relatively small star, such as the sun.

Electromagnetic radiation – Any form of light, ranging from radio waves to gamma rays. Radio waves have the longest wavelength and lowest energy, while gamma rays have the shortest wavelength and highest energy.

Galaxy – A vast system of stars, gas, dust, and other matter held together in space by mutual gravitational pull.

Gravity – The force of attraction that acts between all objects because of their mass. Gravity gives objects on Earth their weight.

Helium – The second simplest chemical element. Helium is produced through the nuclear fusion of hydrogen.

Hydrogen – The simplest chemical element. Hydrogen is the most abundant substance in the universe. It fuels most stars.

Infrared light – A form of light with long wavelengths, also called heat radiation. Infrared is invisible to the human eye.

Kelvin – A metric temperature scale in which zero is absolute zero, the lowest temperature theoretically possible.

Latitude – A measure of the distance between a point on the Earth's surface and the equator.

Light pollution – Artificial light that blots out the faint light of stars.

Light-year – The distance light travels in a vacuum in one year. One light-year is equal to 5.88 trillion miles (9.46 trillion kilometers).

Luminosity – The rate at which a star gives off electromagnetic radiation.

Magnetic field – The force that electric currents exert on other electric currents. A magnetic field causes attraction and repulsion at opposite poles of a magnet.

Magnitude – A measure of the brightness of objects in space. Apparent magnitude is the brightness of a star as seen from Earth. Absolute magnitude is how bright stars would appear if they all were the same distance—32.6 light-years—from Earth.

Mass – The amount of matter in an object.

Neutron star – A star that has collapsed into a small area with extremely high mass. Neutron stars form from the remains of massive stars that have exploded in supernovae.

Nuclear fusion – The combination of two or more atomic nuclei (cores) to form the nucleus of a heavier element. Nuclear fusion releases the energy that powers stars.

Photon – An individual particle of light.

Planet – A large, round heavenly body that orbits a star.

Plasma – A form of matter composed of electrically charged particles that makes up the atmosphere of most stars. A plasma is similar in some respects to a gas, though it usually has a higher temperature.

Prism – A piece of glass that bends light. A prism can break light up into its spectrum.

Radio waves – The form of light with the longest wavelengths. Radio waves are invisible to the human eye.

Red dwarf – A small, relatively cool star that glows with a dim, reddish light. Red dwarfs range in mass from about 1/12 to 1/2 that of the sun.

Red giant – A large, bright star that glows with a reddish light. Red giants range from 10 to 100 times the size of the sun. When its fuel is exhausted, a red giant becomes a white dwarf.

Red supergiant – A huge, extremely bright star that glows with a reddish light. Red supergiants range from 100 to 1,000 times the size of the sun. When its fuel is exhausted, a red supergiant explodes in a supernova.

Solar system – The planetary system that includes the sun and Earth.

Solar wind – The continuous flow of particles given off by the outer atmosphere of the sun.

Spectrum, spectra – Light divided into its different wavelengths. A spectrum may provide astronomers with information about a heavenly body's chemical composition, motion, and distance.

Star – A huge, shining ball in space that produces a tremendous amount of visible light and other forms of energy.

Supernova – An exploding star that can become billions of times as bright as the sun before gradually fading from view. A supernova occurs when a massive star uses up all its fuel.

Ultraviolet light – A form of light with short wavelengths. Ultraviolet light is invisible to the human eye.

Visible light – The form of light human beings can see with their eyes.

Wavelength – The distance between successive crests, or peaks, of a wave. Wavelength is used to distinguish among different forms of light. Radio waves have the longest wavelengths, while gamma rays have the shortest.

White dwarf – A star that has exhausted its fuel. A typical white dwarf has about 60 percent as much mass as the sun, but is no larger than the Earth.

X rays – A form of light with very short wavelengths. X rays are invisible to the human eye.

FOR MORE INFORMATION

WEB SITES

The Constellations and Their Stars

http://www.astro.wisc.edu/~dolan/constellations

Identifies all the constellations and stars by name, by the best months to view them, and by photographs of their position in the sky.

The Cosmic Distance Scale

http://heasarc.gsfc.nasa.gov/docs/cosmic

Zoom out from Earth to the planets and stars, distant galaxies, and beyond to understand how vast our universe is.

Make a Star Finder

http://nasascience.nasa.gov/kids

Enter "constellation finder" in the search box to get NASA's instructions on finding your way around the night sky with a simple device made out of paper.

BOOKS

Find the Constellations
by H. A. Rey (Houghton Mifflin Harcourt, 2008)

Planets, Stars, and Galaxies: A Visual Encyclopedia of Our Universe
by David A. Aguilar (National Geographic Society, 2007)

The Stars: Glowing Spheres in the Sky
by David Jefferis (Crabtree Publishing, 2009)

INDEX

ACKNOWLEDGMENTS

The publishers acknowledge the following sources for illustrations. Credits read from top to bottom, left to right, on their respective pages. All illustrations, maps, charts, and diagrams were prepared by the staff unless otherwise noted.

Cover: NASA/STScI Digitized Sky Survey/Noel Carboni

1   ASA/JPL-Caltech/L. Allen (Harvard-Smithsonian CfA) & Gould's Belt Legacy Team; NASA, H.E. Bond and E. Nelan (Space Telescope Science Institute, Baltimore, Md.)

4-5   NASA, ESA, and the Hubble Heritage (STScI/AURA)-ESA/Hubble Collaboration

6-7   NASA, ESA and Jesús Maíz Apellániz (Instituto de Astrofísica de Andalucía, Spain); NASA/STScI Digitized Sky Survey/Noel Carboni

8-9   © Shutterstock; NASA/CXC/M.Weiss

10-11 European Space Agency & NASA; NASA/JPL-Caltech

12-13 NASA/SOHO; NASA/SOHO; NASA/TRACE; NASA/SOHO; NASA/MSFC; ESO

14-15 NASA/JPL; AP Images; Adolf Schaller/NASA

16-17 WORLD BOOK illustration by Precision Graphics; ESO; © Chuck Eckert, Alamy Images

18-19 © Richard Yandrick, CosmicImage; WORLD BOOK illustration by Don DiSante; NASA, John Krist (Space Telescope Science Institute), Karl Stapelfeldt (Jet Propulsion Laboratory), Jeff Hester (Arizona State University), Chris Burrows (European Space Agency/Space Telescope Science Institute); Jan Robrade/ESA

20-21 NASA/JPL-Caltech; NASA, ESA, A. Fruchter (STScI), and the GOSH Collaboration

22-23 WORLD BOOK illustration by Matt Carrington; © Akira Fujii and David Malin

24-25 © Akira Fujii/DMI; © Akira Fujii/DMI; WORLD BOOK illustration by Amie Zorn/Artisan-Chicago

26-27 Chandra X-ray/NASA/CXC/B.Gaensler et al/ROSAT X-ray; WORLD BOOK illustration by Matt Carrington

28-29 Dan & Cindy Duriscoe, FDSC, Lowell Obs., USNO; Marc Imhoff, NASA GSFC/Christopher Elvidge, NOAA NGDC/Craig Mayhew and Robert Simmon, NASA GSFC

30-31 © Adam Contos/W.M. Keck Observatory; NASA; NASA; NASA; CfAO, Keck Observatory/NSF

32-33 X-ray: NASA/CXC/GSFC/M.Corcoran et al./NASA/STScI

34-35 JAXA, NAOJ, PPARC and NASA; NASA; Dept. of Defense

36-37 © Todd Sladoje; © GIPhotostock/Photo Researchers; © D. Parker, Photo Researchers

38-39 NASA/SOHO; © David Wall, Alamy Images

40-41 WORLD BOOK diagram; NASA/CXC/U.Illinois/R.Williams & Y.H.Chu/NOAO/CTIO/U.Illinois/R.Williams & MCELS coll.; NASA/CXC/MIT/D.Dewey et al., NASA/CXC/SAO/J.DePasquale

42-43 NASA/SOHO; NASA/SOHO; Royal Swedish Academy of Sciences

44-45 NASA/JPL-Caltech/A. Tappe and J. Rho (SSC-Caltech), NASA/CXC/SAO; WORLD BOOK illustration by Matt Carrington; NASA/CXC/SAO/JPL-Caltech/MPIA/Calar Alto, O.Krause et al.

46-47 ASA/JPL-Caltech/L. Allen (Harvard-Smithsonian CfA) & Gould's Belt Legacy Team; NASA, H.E. Bond and E. Nelan (Space Telescope Science Institute, Baltimore, Md.); M. Barstow and M. Burleigh (University of Leicester, U.K.); and J.B. Holberg (University of Arizona)

48-49 © David Malin, UK Schmidt Telescope/DSS/AAO; Granger Collection

50-51 NASA; WORLD BOOK illustration by Matt Carrington

52-53 NASA, ESA, and the Hubble SM4 ERO Team; NASA, ESA, and The Hubble Heritage Team (STScI/AURA); © Stefan Seip

54-55 © Archives Charmet/Bridgeman Art Library; © Erich Lessing/Art Resource; © Werner Forman, Art Resource

56-57 Library of Congress; © Barnaby Norris

58-59 © Asian Art & Archaeology/Corbis; HIP/Art Resource